WHAT'S THE BIG IDEA?

What's the Big Idea? focuses on the hottest issues and ideas around. In a nationwide survey, we asked young people like you to tell us which subjects you find most intriguing, worrying and exciting.
The books in this series tell you what you need to know about the top-rated topics.

Books available now:
The Mind
Virtual Reality
Women's Rights
Animal Rights
The Environment

Books coming soon:
Religion
Time and the Universe
Nuclear Power

We would love to hear what you think. If you would like to make any comments on this book or suggestions for future titles, please write to us at:

What's the Big Idea?
Hodder Children's Books
338 Euston Road
London NW1 3BH

To Venetia, for all your help

Text copyright © Anita Ganeri 1997

The right of Anita Ganeri to be identified as the author of the
Work has been asserted by her in accordance with the Copyright,
Designs and Patents Act 1988.

Illustrations copyright © Andrew McIntyre 1997

Cover illustration by Jake Abrams

Consultant: Bobbi Hoffman, PETA Educational

Published by Hodder Children's Books 1997

10 9 8 7 6 5 4 3 2 1

ISBN 0 340 66720 6

A Catalogue record for this book is available from the
British Library.

Printed by Cox and Wyman Ltd, Reading, Berkshire

Hodder Children's Books
A division of Hodder Headline plc
338 Euston Road
London NW1 3BH

Animal Rights

Anita Ganeri
Illustrated by Andrew McIntyre

Hodder
Children's
Books

a division of Hodder Headline plc

TALKING OF ANIMALS...

Animals have always played a large role in our lives: as working animals; as pets; as food and clothing; as sport and entertainment. And as figures of speech...

Just think of all the sayings and insults we have which feature animals...

at a Snail's Pace

Sick as a Parrot

Dressed up like a Dog's Dinner

Fat as a Pig

Slippery as an Eel

Dead as a DODO

Fit as a Flea

Mutton dressed as Lamb

Butterflies in your Stomach

Hungry enough to eat a Horse

Insults in particular show how some of us view animals. Every time people use an animal term as an insult, e.g. 'cow', 'dog', 'bitch' or 'pig'; they are, however subconsciously, assuming that animals are inferior to humans. Otherwise why would it be an insult to be compared to them?

This is called **speciesism*** - where humans discriminate against animals, classing them as a 'lower' species in the pecking order.

If animals could talk, it's anyone's guess what *they'd* say about *us*!

* See Glossary

It wasn't always this way. In Ancient Egypt, many animals were seen as superior. Egyptian gods were often associated with particular animals, and shown in carvings and paintings with the head of that animal to make them easier to recognise. The animals themselves were often considered sacred in their own right.

Anubis (jackal-headed) - god of the dead and embalming
Sekhmet (lioness) - goddess of motherhood
Set (donkey or hippo) - god of deserts and storms
Bast (cat) - goddess of healing
Sobek (crocodile) - god of water
Thoth (baboon) - god of wisdom

More Pillows!

FACT FLASH: The Ancient Egyptians were great cat lovers. The penalty for killing a cat was death!

The way in which different societies treat animals often reflects their different religious and moral beliefs.

One of the most important beliefs for Hindus and Buddhists is *ahimsa*, or non-violence. This means that they don't believe in harming or killing living things, so many are vegetarian. In Hindu society, the cow, in particular, is sacred, because it provides life-giving milk.

> The greatness of a nation and its moral progress can be measured by the way its animals are treated.

Mahatma Gandhi (1869-1948)
(Indian political and spiritual leader)

In the West, religion was more likely to place *mankind* above the animals. Think of the Garden of Eden. Who was blamed for Adam and Eve's downfall? A serpent, that's who! And what about Noah? Sure the animals went in two by two, but you can bet that Noah was boss!

The Bible says that man 'has dominion over every living thing' emphasising this role at the top of the hierachy. But if man is top dog, how far should the other animals be used for his own ends? This was something that no one seemed to agree on.

To our ancestors, animal rights meant nothing. After all, what on Earth was the point of mammoths, if you couldn't hunt and eat them?

In the first century AD, Greek writer, Plutarch, was one of the first to speak out on behalf of animals. He was appalled by the Roman wild beast shows, saying: *"Kindness and benevolence should be extended to creatures of every species."*

But his views were not widely shared.

In the thirteenth century, St Francis of Assisi said, *"Not to hurt our humble brethren is our first duty to them, but to stop there is not enough. We have a higher mission - to be of service to them wherever they require it."*

But for centuries, the Christian church refused to acknowledge that human beings had any moral responsibility towards animals. It still held the view that animals had been put on Earth simply to be useful to us.

For thousands of years, people all over the world have put animals to work. Before the invention of mechanised ploughs and tractors, fields were ploughed by teams of oxen, horses or buffalo. Farmers in some countries, such as India, still use animal-drawn ploughs because money is tight and an animal is often cheaper to keep than a tractor. Donkeys, mules, yaks, camels and other so-called 'beasts of burden' were, and still are, used throughout the world to transport goods and people.

So, what do animals mean to *you*? How do you 'use' animals?

Here are some examples of different ways we 'use' animals. Can you think of any more?

• **Working animals**

Sheep dogs
Guide dogs for the blind/deaf
Police sniffer dogs
Beasts of burden
(e.g. donkeys, mules,
yaks, camels)

• **Animals as food**

Meat (e.g. turkey breast,
frog's legs, chicken wings,
leg of lamb)
Dairy products
(e.g. eggs, milk, cheese,
cream, butter)

• **Companion animals/pets**

Domestic pets (e.g. cats, dogs)
Exotic pets
(e.g. snakes, turtles, macaws)
School pets
(e.g. hamsters, gerbils)

• In sport and entertainment

Horse racing
Greyhound racing
Showjumping
Bullfighting
Zoos and circuses
Films

• Animal experiments

(e.g. on rats, mice, rabbits, chimps)
Cosmetic testing
Drug testing
Organ transplants
Psychological testing
(e.g. on chimps, macaque monkeys)

• Clothes from animals

Leather (e.g. cows)
Wool (e.g. sheep, yaks)
Fur (e.g. seal, mink, beaver)
Silk (e.g. silk worms)

100%
BEAVER
HOT
WATER
BOTTLE

Today, more and more of the jobs previously done by animals are being done by machines. Most working animals in Britain nowadays are dogs - sheepdogs, guide dogs, guard dogs and police dogs, trained to sniff out drugs and explosives.

Some people believe that *however* we use animals, we are, in fact, abusing them.

For example, many people think that training animals to perform circus tricks is cruel and degrading to the animals. But the same people might well praise police dogs which have been trained to sniff out drugs or help find earthquake victims buried under piles of rubble.

So, what's the difference?

Are these animals simply valuable for their usefulness, as you would value a machine, and nothing more? Or should they, as living things, be treated with respect and even affection?

The French philosopher, René Descartes (1596-1650) declared all animals to be no better than machines because he believed they had no soul, and no power to reason or have conscious thoughts.

I don't know, but I think I prefer the old Cat.....

He thought that animals were only valuable while they were useful, and, however much we feel our attitudes towards animals have changed, this is still a widespread view today. For example, lab animals are often killed after the experiments they take part in are finished; race horses are put down if they break a leg; and greyhounds too are often put down at the end of their working lives - normally when they are just three years old (their natural life span is fourteen years) - instead of being allowed to grow old gracefully.

The idea of animals as machines is clear when we look at the development of **factory farming** - with animals as the machines and meat as the product - or at **vivisection** (the practice of experimenting upon live animals).

The first vivisectionists experimented on animals without anaesthetic, believing the creatures could feel no pain, because they were incapable of thought and feeling.

CHANGING ATTITUDES

A greater awareness of animal rights began to emerge in the sixteenth and seventeenth centuries, in the writings of many European scholars. And, when it was discovered that the physical make-up of an animal and a human was very similar, protests began to be made.

The French writer, Voltaire, questioned Descartes' views.

Has Nature arranged all the springs of feeling in this animal to the end that he might not feel? Has he nerves that he may be incapable of suffering?

Voltaire (1694-1778)

And Jeremy Bentham (1748-1832), the English philosopher, wrote: *"The question is not Can they reason? nor Can they talk? but Can they suffer?"*. He believed that animals should be treated with the same respect and responsibility as human beings.

By the late eighteenth and early nineteenth centuries, the rights of *all* living things, human and animal, began to receive more attention. This concern was sparked by mounting opposition to the slave trade - which was finally abolished in the 1860s - and concern for women's rights, particularly their campaign to win the vote. John Stuart Mill and William Wilberforce, campaigners in both these areas, were also prime movers in pushing for a law to protect animals.

The reasons for legal intervention... apply not less strongly to the case of those unfortunate slaves and victims of the most brutal part of mankind - the lower animals.

At last, in 1822, the British Parliament passed the first ever **animal welfare** law - the Act to Prevent the Cruel and Improper Treatment of Cattle. It became an offence to 'beat, abuse, or ill-treat cruelly and for no reason any horse, donkey, cow or sheep'. The maximum penalty for breaking the law was two years' imprisonment.

Two years later, in 1824, the Society for the Prevention of Cruelty to Animals (which later became the RSPCA) was founded.

Animals rights were here to stay!

Some people still firmly believed that animals were inferior to human beings. But one crucial thing had slipped their minds - HUMANS ARE ANIMALS TOO!

The man responsible for bringing this startling fact to light was the English naturalist, Charles Darwin. In his two famous works, *The Origin of the Species* and *The Descent of Man*, Darwin set out his theory that humans were descended from apes.

Man in his arrogance thinks himself a great work, worthy of a deity. More humble, and, I believe, true, to consider him created from animals.

DO NOT FEED THE ANIMALS

Charles Darwin (1809-1892)

It caused a sensation and many people were deeply insulted, refusing point-blank to believe any such thing. They maintained that people were created by God.

So - *do* animals have rights? And, if we believe that they do, how far should we respect these rights? Where do we draw the line if we care about animals? At eating meat? At wearing leather? At keeping pets? Can we *ever* use animals for our own ends without abusing them?

Animal <u>rights</u> campaigners believe that *all* animals have the moral right to be treated with respect and without exploitation. At their most extreme, they believe in the total abolition of animal use of any kind, including keeping pets.

Animal <u>welfare</u> campaigners concentrate on seeking the best possible conditions for, and treatment of, animals. They recognise that, while you can't stop the use of animals, you *can* stop or reduce the abuse.

THE GREAT DEBATE

Do animals have rights?

YES!

- Animals are living, sentient (feeling) beings, just like humans. They feel pain, fear, pleasure and hunger, just like humans.
- If humans have rights, animals should have them too.
- Animals lives are as important to them as ours are to us.
- It is wrong to treat animals simply as tools, machine-substitutes or as slaves.
- It is wrong to exploit *all* animals, including humans.

Do animals have rights?

NO!

- Humans are superior to other animals because they can speak, reason and learn.
- Rights are a human concept and therefore only apply to humans. They are irrelevant to animals.
- As superior beings, humans have the right to use and exploit animals for their own ends.
- Human rights should be our main concern, not animal rights.

What do YOU think?

QUICK QUIZ

If you're not sure *what* you think, why not try this quick quiz? There aren't any right or wrong answers but it should get you thinking. Try it again when you've read the rest of the book - you might be surprised!

1. (a)   Which animal do you like best?

   (b)   Which do you like least?

Can you think of five reasons why?

BEAR IN MIND I AM WEARING GLASSES!

2.   If you had to make one of these animals extinct, which would it be?
   a)   dog
   b)   chimpanzee
   c)   spider
   d)   magpie
   e)   leech
   f)   shark

3.   A new medicine is being developed. Are you prepared to act as a human guinea-pig, so that it doesn't have to be tested on animals?

4.   Which animal rights issue do you think is the most important? For example, factory farming, live animal exports, zoos, animal experiments.

5. Which of the following would you eat?

a) chicken
b) tuna fish
c) frog
d) dog
e) pig (pork)
f) cow (beef)
g) none of the above

6. Would you buy cosmetics which had not been tested on animals, even if they were more expensive?

7. Do you have a pet? Would you be upset if it died?

8. Do you think killing an animal is ever justified? Have you ever swatted a fly or a mosquito?

9. Do you wear clothes made from leather (e.g. shoes, jacket)? Would you, under any circumstances, wear fur?

10. What would you do if you saw someone being cruel to an animal?

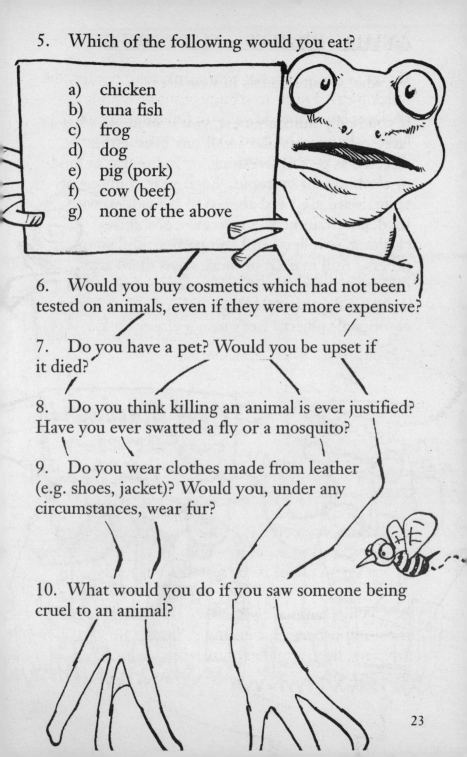

ANIMAL RIGHTS – THE ISSUES

So, what about animals in *your* life?

If you really think about it, you'll soon see what a large role animals play in all our lives: either directly, as pets or livestock, or indirectly, as food or clothing, for example. Each year, millions of animals are used and abused to provide us with food, entertainment, medicines, cosmetics, clothing, jewellery, and companionship, amongst others. And in each of these areas there are different concerns, different points of view and different depths of feeling - animal rights is an emotional subject. Let's take a closer look...

OLD MACDONALD HAD A FARM...

Think of a farm. What do you see? Rolling fields with swaying stalks of corn? Sheep grazing? A large stone farmhouse with chickens scratching in the yard? Think again! Some farms are like your idyllic picture. Many are very different indeed.

It all began after the Second World War when farmers were asked to produce more and more food for a new, wealthier society. To start with, it was great for animals - suddenly they had proper shelter and decent food - but, as farmers spent more money on their businesses, they realised they had to get more for their money - and started working the animals harder, which meant conditions went downhill.

Each year in Britain alone, 750 million animals are killed for food - not including dairy cattle and laying hens (hens kept for their eggs).

Many spend their whole, short lives in dark, cramped indoor pens or cages, being fed, watered and fattened up for slaughter. It's like an animal version of a factory production line - that's why it's called factory farming. You'll remember Descartes' comparison of animals with machines. Well, in factory farming, that's just how they're treated.

Factory Farming

The <u>advantage</u> of factory farming is that farmers can produce more meat, eggs or milk more cheaply, to fuel the demand for cheap, quality food. It's a very intensive method of farming, raising the largest number of animals in the smallest space.

The <u>disadvantage</u> is that animals are seen simply as food machines. They are kept in conditions which deprive them of even their basic behavioural needs and their lives are short and miserable.

FACTORY FRESH EGGS 50p

So, What Are The Alternatives?

Free-range farming - this means that the animals are allowed to roam freely in the fresh air where they can behave normally, with access to grass and protection from the elements.

Organic farming - this is where food is produced as naturally as possible, without the use of chemical pesticides or fertilisers. Animals are fed only on organically produced food. You can buy organic meat and milk, as well as fruit and vegetables.

The **advantage** of organic/free-range farming is that the consumer (you!) knows that the animal concerned has been treated as humanely as possible and has been able to express normal behaviour, free from pain or distress.

The **disadvantage** of organic/free range farming is that these products are less widely available and cost more to produce than factory farmed goods, because they are less intensive, i.e. less animals to more space. And this additional cost has to be passed on to the customer, so organic products are often expensive.

Quack!

Cattle Conundrum

Where would we be without them? They give us milk, meat, leather... and cowpats. And many are well looked after. But not all...

- **Dairy cows** - to produce milk, a dairy cow must have a calf each year. So the dairy cow has a double burden - for much of her five to six years of life (a cow's natural lifespan is about twenty years), she's pregnant and being milked. Some modern dairy breeds produce 50 litres of milk a day - ten times the amount needed to suckle a calf.

As a result, many dairy cows suffer from:

- *Mastitis*, a painful infection of the udders (because they are producing so much milk and because of hormones injected into them to increase their yields).
- *Acidosis*, or acid in the stomach (because they are fed high protein feed to increase their milk yields).
- *Lameness* of hind feet and hooves (because their udders are so large they cannot walk properly and because of the cramped conditions they live in).

- **Beef cattle** - these are specially bred or taken from the dairy herd. Calves reared intensively are often housed completely indoors while they are fattened up. They are slaughtered for their lean meat when they are between ten and fifteen months old.

- **Veal calves** - every year, hundreds of thousands of calves are sent abroad to countries such as the Netherlands, Belgium and France for veal production. The calves are taken from their mothers at three days old and kept in tiny, dark crates where they are fed on a liquid-only diet until they are sent for slaughter at twelve to fourteen weeks. The restricted space prevents the animals developing muscle through exercise and the liquid diet prevents them putting on fat. Their meat is therefore lean and white, and eaten as a delicacy in many countries. This system is considered so cruel that it was banned in Britain in 1990. Campaigners want it banned throughout Europe and the U.S.

A Pig Problem

There are about 8 million pigs in Britain and they're mainly reared for pork, bacon, ham and sausages. Like other factory-farmed animals, they're kept in cramped, intensive conditions until it's time for them to be fattened up for slaughter.

When it comes to pigs, the main animal rights concerns are:
- Sows (female pigs) are tied to racks or stalls for mating.
- Almost as soon as one litter of piglets is weaned, a sow is mated again. So, she spends at least two-thirds of her life pregnant.
- About half of all breeding sows are kept inside in metal-barred sow stalls or tethered with an iron chain. For four months of pregnancy, the sows cannot turn round or walk backwards or forwards. These stalls will be banned from 1998.

- A week before giving birth, sows are moved to small farrowing crates where they stay for two to four weeks until the piglets are weaned. The sow has no room to turn round, but farmers claim the crates stop the sow squashing her new-born piglets.

- The cramped, crowded conditions lead to a variety of diseases, especially in piglets. These include viral pneumonia, meningitis, blue-ear disease, porcine stress syndrome (PSS) and behavioural problems.

Pig breeding is big business, with modern breeds specially developed for faster growth, leaner meat and larger litters of piglets. This causes its own problems. But many pig farmers are responding to people's concerns and changing to free-range or 'freer' indoor breeding methods.

WHICH CAME FIRST
The Chicken or the Egg?

Meanwhile, down on the free-range farm, things are rather different...

Egg-laying Hens - The Facts

- The vast majority of egg-laying hens are kept in tiny, cramped battery cages, with no room to stretch their wings and nowhere to roost or nest. The average wingspan of a hen is 82 cm, while the average cage is only 46 cm x 51 cm - and that's for at least four birds, so you can imagine how cramped it is. The cages them selves are stacked up to six tiers high in a huge, windowless shed.

- Each **battery hen** has a living space only about three times the size of this page. Think of three people crammed into a telephone box and you've got the picture!

- As a result, hens suffer from damaged feet and claws, and extremely brittle bones, among other things.

- Chicks are often 'debeaked' to stop them pecking each other. The tips of their beaks are sliced off with a red-hot knife, causing long-lasting pain.

- The battery cage method is the cheapest way of producing eggs. And, because feeding and egg collection are done automatically, one person can look after as many as 50,000 hens in a single building.

Broiler Hens - The Facts

- Broiler hens are chickens bred for meat.
- To produce meat cheaply and quickly, tens of thousands of hens are crammed into huge sheds and fed on high energy diets amd antibiotics to gain weight fast.
- This abnormally fast growth rate (twice normal) causes painful leg problems and bone deformities.
- Diseases, such as salmonella, spread quickly through the densely-packed flocks.
- You can buy free-range chicken, but it is more expensive.

And what about geese? Did you know that pâté de foie gras, a great delicacy in some places, is made by force feeding geese through tubes with about 2.5 kg of grain a day, every day, for three to four weeks? When they are eventually slaughtered, their livers (from which the pâté is made) weigh over one hundred times more than a normal goose liver. It's like you being made to eat 12.5 kg of spaghetti a day for three weeks non-stop! Horrible.

FASTER THERE, BOY!

SPAGHETTI

LIVE ANIMAL EXPORTS

It's emotional, controversial and a fierce campaign has been fought to put an end to it, with people from all walks of life taking part in protests, even putting themselves at risk to stop exports taking place. We're talking about LIVE ANIMAL EXPORTS. Here are some things you should know.

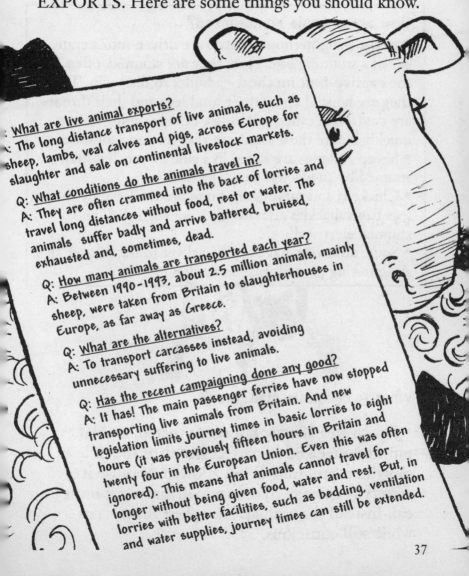

Q: What are live animal exports?

A: The long distance transport of live animals, such as sheep, lambs, veal calves and pigs, across Europe for slaughter and sale on continental livestock markets.

Q: What conditions do the animals travel in?

A: They are often crammed into the back of lorries and travel long distances without food, rest or water. The animals suffer badly and arrive battered, bruised, exhausted and, sometimes, dead.

Q: How many animals are transported each year?

A: Between 1990-1993, about 2.5 million animals, mainly sheep, were taken from Britain to slaughterhouses in Europe, as far away as Greece.

Q: What are the alternatives?

A: To transport carcasses instead, avoiding unnecessary suffering to live animals.

Q: Has the recent campaigning done any good?

A: It has! The main passenger ferries have now stopped transporting live animals from Britain. And new legislation limits journey times in basic lorries to eight hours (it was previously fifteen hours in Britain and twenty four in the European Union. Even this was often ignored). This means that animals cannot travel for longer without being given food, water and rest. But, in lorries with better facilities, such as bedding, ventilation and water supplies, journey times can still be extended.

LAMBS TO THE SLAUGHTER...

Millions of animals are slaughtered every day for meat. Whilst there are rules and regulations controlling where and how slaughter takes place, controversy still surrounds current slaughter methods.

How are animals slaughtered?

• In the slaughterhouse, cattle are driven into a crate, called a stunning box. Here they are stunned, often by the **captive-bolt method** - a bullet to the brain. Then they are hoisted up by their hind legs and their throats are cut (this is called **sticking**). Sticking must follow quickly before the animal can recover consciousness.

• Sheep and pigs are killed in a similar way but may be stunned by an electric shock instead.

• Chickens and turkeys are hung upside down by their legs from shackles attached to a conveyor belt and stunned electrically.

• Some **abattoirs** have an official vet to watch over all slaughtering procedures. Some don't.

What is religious slaughter?

• Jewish and Islamic law states that an animal must be alive and in perfect health at the time of slaughter. Stunning is not allowed, because it counts as damage to the animal, making it unfit to eat. Instead the animals have their throats cut while still conscious.

• Cattle killed by this method are restrained in an upright pen, prior to slaughter. Sheep are either slaughtered on their backs in a sort of cradle, restrained by their feet or hoisted off the ground by their back legs before the cut is made.

• A trained rabbi carries out the slaughtering for those of the Jewish faith, using a knife whose sharpness must meet official guidelines.

• In the Muslim method (called *Halal*), any adult male can carry out the slaughtering, with or without training.

It's a very sharp knife!

How can slaughter be made more humane?

• There is concern that present stunning methods aren't always reliable and that a third of animals may still be conscious when their throats are cut.

• Some campaigners recommend the use of carbon dioxide gas to put animals to sleep instead.

• Local authorities must enforce current welfare and hygiene laws concerning the slaughter of animals.

• Slaughterhouse staff must be properly trained in animal handling and welfare.

• Plans are under way to design a mobile slaughterhouse. Animals could then be killed on the farm rather than suffer the stress of being transported further away to an abattoir.

But... i'm an Atheist!

• A study of religious slaughter recommended that stunning or partial stunning of the animal should be carried out before slaughter - but this has yet to be agreed.

IS MEAT MURDER?

If you'd tried to tell a caveman that eating mammoths was wrong, he'd have laughed in your face!

It was meat or nothing in those days - you hunted to survive. Today, however, there is more choice than ever before. Many people are giving up meat and going vegetarian.

Are you what you eat?

• **Vegetarian** - this term was introduced in 1847 when the Vegetarian Society was founded and means someone who does not eat meat, fish or poultry. Vegetarians eat grains, pulses, vegetables, fruit, nuts and seeds. They also eat eggs (free range) and dairy products because these do not involve the slaughter of animals. They avoid foods made with animal products, such as cheese made with rennet from a calf's stomach, and choose cheese made with vegetarian rennet instead.

A large proportion of vegetarians believe that killing animals for food is wrong, and are concerned about the suffering these animals go through on the way to our tables.

• **Vegan** - someone who takes vegetarianism a step further. Vegans avoid *all* animal produce, including milk, eggs and honey. They are against animal exploitation of any kind, whether for food, clothing, cosmetics or entertainment. They don't wear leather or use products tested on animals.

BUT

• Some people care deeply about animal welfare while still eating meat.
• And some non-vegetarians argue that the animals in question are reared specifically for food. Otherwise they wouldn't be alive in the first place. Many are concerned that animals are humanely slaughtered and do not suffer while they are alive. They make sure they buy products that guarantee this, but see no reason not to eat the end product.

You have to do what's best for you.

The Wider Issues

Many people are also concerned about the wider implications of meat production. Here are some of the key areas of concern.

Q: What is Mad Cow Disease?
A: Its real name is Bovine Spongiform Encephalopathy (BSE, for short) and it's a fatal brain disease seen in cattle. It's caused by feeding animal offal, e.g. cattle and sheep brains, to cows.

Cows are meant to eat GRASS! Tampering with the food chain is NOT a good idea, and this practice is now banned. Recently, a very similar disease (called Creutzfeldt-Jakob Disease, or CJD) has been blamed for several human deaths. They may have been caused by eating beef contaminated with BSE. No one knows for sure.

Q: Is wearing leather cruel?
A: Leather and suede are made from the hides of animals slaughtered for their meat, so is indirectly part of a cruel process. In fact, about 30% of slaughterhouse profits come from the leather industry, so wearing leather means buying into something you might not particularly want to be involved in. For this reason, many vegetarians and vegans avoid leather shoes, bags, belts and so on. Others argue that the animals would be killed anyway and it would be wasteful not to put their hides to good use. They are also concerned about the practice of using environmentally unfriendly plastics as alternative materials.

Q: What about other by-products of slaughter?
A: Many foods contain ingredients derived from the slaughter of animals, making them unsuitable for vegetarians. For instance, wine gums, marsh-mallows and jellies contain gelatine, made from boiled animal bones, tendons and ligaments. Many foods, including cakes, biscuits and margarine, also contain animal fats.

Q: Is meat production bad for the environment?

A: Yes, it is! Vast areas of tropical rainforest have been destroyed to make room for commercial cattle ranches. In Central America alone, 90% of the forest has been cleared for cattle ranching. And after just a few years, the cattle are moved on. What a waste.

Q: Can you be vegetarian and eat fish?

A: No! Vegetarians and vegans count fishing as another type of animal abuse, where fish and shellfish are taken from their natural habitat and killed, often cruelly, to feed humans (some, like lobsters, are boiled alive). People are also concerned about over-fishing, running down breeding stocks and threatening some species with extinction through the use of drift nets.

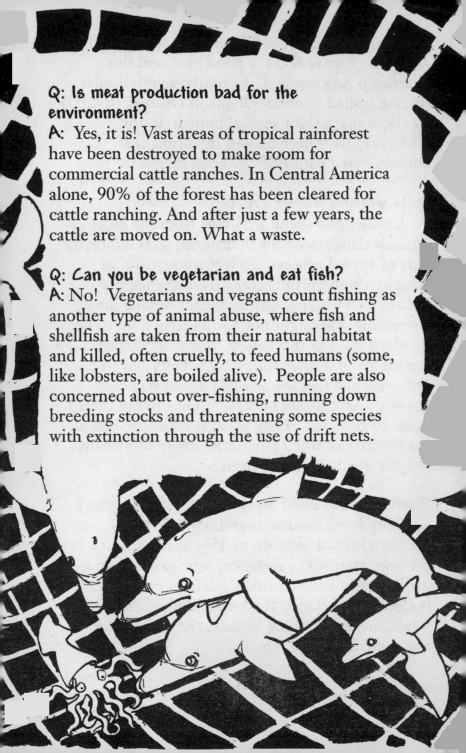

What do these people have in common?

Mahatma Gandhi
The Buddha
Leonardo da Vinci
Leo Tolstoy
George Bernard Shaw
Adolf Hitler
Charles Darwin
Sir Isaac Newton
Albert Einstein
Percy Bysshe Shelley
Brigitte Bardot
Paul McCartney

Tina Turner
Joanna Lumley
Damon Albarn
David Bowie
Martina Navratilova
Victoria Wood
Boy George
Kim Basinger
Michael Jackson
Annie Lennox
Michael Stipe
David Duchovny

Animals are my friends... and I don't eat my friends.

I AGREE, BUT THEN AGAIN, YOU DID FORGET MY BIRTHDAY!

George Bernard Shaw (Irish playwright. 1856-1950)

Answer: They are or were all famous vegetarians or vegans.

What's For Dinner?

Attitudes to eating animals vary enormously around the world. Some of the things on this menu may make *your* toes curl, but in the countries where they are eaten, they are considered perfectly acceptable. And it's not just far-flung or exotic places, either. Take haggis, for example!

menu

- Frogs' legs - France
- Snake steak - South East Asia
- Witchetty grubs - Australia
- Live monkey brain - Hong Kong
- Sheep eyeballs - Arabia
- Dog - China and Korea
- Boiled cat - China and Korea
- Locusts - Africa
- Bear cub - South East Asia

FACT FLASH: In Chinese culture, any animal that has its back towards heaven can be eaten. Dogs and cats are considered warming winter food and other animals are eaten for their special properties, such as owls, to improve eyesight.

DANGER: WILDLIFE!

Wild animals worldwide are being wiped out by the greed and commercial activities of human beings. In the short-term, rewards are great, but they don't last long. Once an animal is extinct, however, it's gone forever - a very long time indeed.

10 REASONS WHY ANIMALS ARE IN DANGER

1) Killed for the table - eating endangered species is a status symbol in some places.

2) Killed as pests - in Australia, for instance, farmers shoot millions of kangaroos a year as vermin, and now they're targeting cats!

3) Killed when their habitat is destroyed - on purpose. Remember the rainforests? Cattle ranching's one thing but huge areas of forest are also cut down to make living space for the ranchers, and for farms, mines and roads.

4) Killed when their habitat is destroyed - by accident. In February 1996, the tanker *Sea Empress* ran aground off the Welsh coast. A staggering 72,500 tonnes of oil leaked into the sea. The victims? Some 1,300 sq km of sea, 200 km of coastline and thousands of birds, fish and sea creatures. Much of the shoreline may never recover.

5) Captured for the trade in exotic pets (e.g. parrots and macaws).
6) Captured or bred for use in laboratory research and experiments (e.g. chimps and monkeys).
7) Killed to make luxury goods (e.g. from furs, skins and ivory) and tourist souvenirs.
8) Killed for the Chinese medicine trade.
9) Killed for damaging crops (e.g. African elephants).
10) Killed because of local fears and taboos (e.g. Madagascan aye-ayes, Indian tigers).

Buying and selling animals is big business. Much of which is legal and above board. But it's the illegal trade in endangered species that's the problem. Despite international rules and regulations, many rare animals face extinction if the poachers and traders aren't stopped. Can you imagine a world without tigers? You might not have long to wait.

FACT FLASH: The illegal international wildlife trade is worth about £4 billion a year!

CITES Needs You!

The Convention on International Trade in Endangered Species of Wild Fauna and Flora (CITES, for short) was set up in 1975. It now has 122 member countries and governs the worldwide commercial trade in some 35,000 species of animals and plants currently in danger of **extinction**. Species are put into three categories, called Appendices:

• APPENDIX 1: Species threatened with extinction and listed as **endangered**. All international commercial trade in these species is banned.

• APPENDIX II: Species not currently threatened with extinction but which may become so unless their trade is carefully controlled. Trade is only allowed if it does not threaten their survival.

• APPENDIX III: Allows member countries to list species which are protected only by their own national laws and to ask for co-operation in controlling their trade.

But does it work?

Because the trade in endangered species is illegal (and very valuable), it is extremely hard to control. Animals are transported with faked, official papers, or smuggled in suitcases and secret compartments - all difficult to detect. And fines and punishments are tricky to enforce. But it's much, much better than nothing!

A Case In Point - Five Threatened Species

Endangered means an animal is in danger of extinction and unlikely to survive unless steps are taken to save it.

1. MINKE WHALE
Distribution: North Atlantic Ocean
Numbers in the wild: c. 53,000
Threat: Trade in whale meat
Main consumers: Japan,
Iceland, Norway
Status: CITES Appendix 1

2. QUEEN ALEXANDRA'S
BIRDWING BUTTERFLY
Distribution: Papua New Guinea
Threat: International
butterfly collectors
Main consumers: Japan,
Europe, USA
Status: CITES Appendix 1

3. AFRICAN ELEPHANT
Distribution: Africa, south
of the Sahara Desert
Numbers in the wild:
c. 600,000
Threat: Poaching for ivory
and hides, orphaned calves
captured for zoos and circuses.
Status: CITES Appendix 1

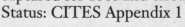

4. ASIATIC LION

Distribution: Gir Forest, India
Numbers in the wild: c. 250-300
Threat: Disease and overpopulation have brought the lions into conflict with local people, as the villages encroach on their natural habitat. The lions are killed to protect the locals.
Status: CITES Appendix 1

5. BLACK RHINO

Distribution: Central and southern Africa
Numbers in the wild: c. 2,000
Threat: Trade in horns for Chinese medicine (£2.8 million worth of rhino horn was seized in Britain in 1996, representing 1% of the world population of rhino).
Main consumers: South East Asia
Status: CITES Appendix 1

FACT FLASH: Britain's attempts to protect certain of its own indigenous species have been so successful (250,000 badgers in the UK in 1996, compared to 100,000 in 1966) that some formerly endangered animals are now treated as pests and are culled in some areas (i.e. killed off to keep numbers down).

The Primate Trade

One of the worst examples of the illegal wildlife trade is the trade in primates (apes and monkeys). These intelligent, sensitive and sociable animals are beaten and drugged to make them easier to catch, and mothers are killed so their babies can be snatched. They then endure appalling journeys, cooped up in tiny crates. The vast majority never make it.

So, where do the primates end up?

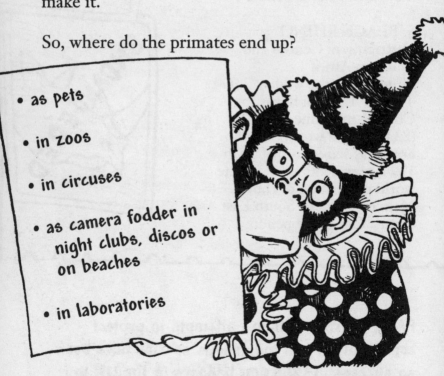

- as pets

- in zoos

- in circuses

- as camera fodder in night clubs, discos or on beaches

- in laboratories

Conditions are often atrocious and the animals' lives short and miserable. Many die in transit, from disease or starvation. Others face a life of boredom and stress, away from their family groups and natural habitats.

What can be done?

• The IPPL (International Primate Protection League) was founded in 1971. It uses a network of overseas agents to track down and expose illegal traders and smugglers.
• On some Spanish beaches, tourists can be photographed with chimps. You can help by not being one of them.
• Most primate species are covered by CITES. But with live chimps fetching about £15,000 each in research laboratories, the rules are often broken. Chimpanzees are now threatened with extinction, even though trade in them has been banned for some 20 years.

53

Is Killing Or Capture Ever Justified?

Some people think it is.

"YES! We live near the tiger reserve. Sometimes the tigers come into the village. They haven't attacked anyone yet, but if they did, we'd have to kill them. We also need to go into the forest to collect firewood and food. Why should the tigers be so well looked after when we don't get enough to eat?"
(Farmer, India)

"NO! Since 1930, tiger numbers have fallen from 40,000 to only about 2,500 in 1996. And they will continue to fall as long as villages keep expanding into their forest habitat and as long as they are poached for their skins and bones (for Chinese medicine). Unless special reserves are set aside for Indian tigers, they will become extinct."

"YES! Last year, we shot three hundred elephants for ecological reasons in a single cull. They were destroying the trees in the park. I mean, what hope does a tree have against a 4-tonne elephant?"
(Park-ranger, South Africa)

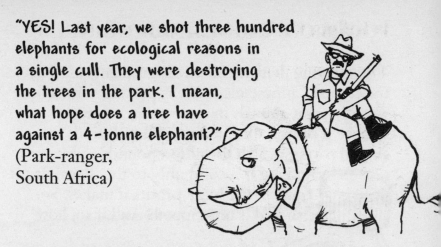

"NO! Elephants are vital to the well-being of the African bush. If one park can't support them all, some should be moved to another park."

"YES! We've been killing pilot whales for over four hundred years. It's part of our culture. Whale meat's a big part of our diet."
(Fisherman, Faroe Islands)

"NO! The Faroe Islands (part of Denmark) enjoy a high standard of living and do not need to kill whales for food. Hundreds of whales are killed each year and much of the meat and blubber (fat) goes to waste. Also, the slaughter methods used cause unnecessary suffering – the whales are driven towards the beach and hacked to death."

FOCUS ON: CHINESE MEDICINE

The growing demand for the ingredients used in traditional Chinese medicine is putting some of the world's rarest animals in even greater danger. Believe it or not, this lucrative (illegal) trade in animal parts is worth £3 billion pounds a year, ranking it second only to the illegal drugs trade in the huge profits it makes. So, should it be stopped? And if so, how?

Some facts and figures:

GENERAL MALADY
miracle Syrup
Bears' gall bladder
Bear bile
Powdered rhino horn
Powered tiger bones
Tiger penis
Saiga antelope horn
Dried centipede
Dried seahorse
Extract of cobra
Powdered turtleshell

• Medicines made with rhino or saiga antelope horn are used to reduce fevers, fits and headaches.
• Some 10,000 bears are kept on Chinese bear farms and 'milked' through tubes for the bile in their stomachs. Many live in appalling conditions, in tiny metal cages. There are international calls for such farms to be banned.
• Bear bile is used to treat many ailments, from burns, to liver and eye diseases, to cancer. Herbal alternatives are available.
• The going rate for bear gall bladder is £2000–£3000 per kg.
• Powdered turtleshell is used to treat anything from a sore throat to the pain of childbirth.

Conservation versus Tradition - the dilemma

"When Chinese medicine began, there were plenty of animals to go round. But times have changed. Rhinos, tigers and Asian bears all now face extinction if the laws are not enforced. Compromise is the only way forward - to allow people to trade legally, keeping trade off the black market and out in the open where it can be properly controlled. We've got to persuade people it's in their best interests. If the animals die out, so does Chinese medicine."

"Traditional Chinese medicine is ancient - about 2000 years old. Millions of people rely on it. They're suspicious of Western medicine. Besides, many of them can't afford it. The Chinese resent Westerners trying to tell them what they can and can't do. They see the conservationists as a threat not only to their medicine but to their culture too."

FACT FLASH: Did you know that Russia's brown bear is now under such threat from the Chinese medicine trade that the species is protected by armed police?

NO SKIN OFF YOUR BACK!

Each year, some 25 million wild animals are trapped for their fur. A further 45 million are raised on **fur farms**. There is also a growing black-market trade in the furs of endangered species. On the one hand, the fur trade is a worldwide industry worth millions of pounds. On the other, it's outdated, barbaric and unnecessary. Which is it?

Q: Which animals are killed for their fur?
A: Beavers, raccoons, foxes, mink, lynx and other wild cats. Endangered species include jaguars, snow leopards, tigers and ocelots.

Q: How are they killed?
A: In the wild, steel-jawed leghold traps are laid which catch any animals that wanders by. These traps cause excruciating pain and suffering - like having a car door slammed shut on your fingers. Animals can lie in agony for several days before the trapper finds them - sometimes biting off their own paws to escape. Many countries have now banned these traps. Mink and foxes are raised on fur farms, then either electrocuted or gassed to death.

Q: How many animals go into making one fur coat?
A: 1 fur coat = 20 beavers or 40 mink or 200 chinchillas.

Q: Is wearing fur necessary or plain vain?
A: People, such as the Inuit of the Arctic, have long worn animal fur and skins as protection against the bitter cold. But for most people in the world, particularly in the West, furs are luxury clothes, unnecessary for survival and worn largely for show.

Q: What do the fur traders say about all this?
A: They argue that trapping actually helps to control wild animal populations before they become pests, that fur farming isn't cruel, and that if animals weren't considered commercially valuable, they'd be at even greater risk of extinction.

Q: Are there any man-made alternatives to fur?
A: There are. But avoid fake furs - they look like the real thing and give out the wrong message. For keeping warm in winter, get a fleecy jacket.

Q: Has the campaigning done any good?
A: Yes, it has. Groups such as Lynx and PETA (People for the Ethical Treatment of Animals) have succeeded in changing public opinion with high-profile campaigns. Two thirds of people in Britain now think it's wrong to kill animals for their fur. And many fur traders and farms have been put out of business. But the picture is far from clear. PETA claim that 1993 figures show that fur sales have dropped by 50% since the late 1980s, while The Fur Education Council insists that sales were up by 30% in Britain in 1995 and some international fashion designers, such as Gucci and Fendi, are already beginning to reintroduce fur into their ranges.

Match The Goods To The Animals

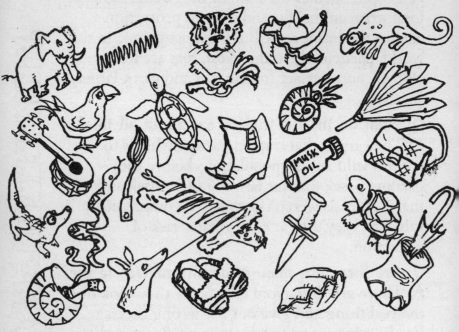

Umbrella stand	musk deer
Fly whisk	elephant
Cowboy boots	turtle
Handbag and purse	caiman
Ivory chess set	tiger
Tortoiseshell brush and comb	snake
Shell ashtray	nautilus turtle
Guitar	Spix macaw
Feather fan	tiger
Fruit bowl	chameleon
Knife with horn handle	rhino
Bottle of musk oil	elephant
Tiger skin rug	giant clam
Key rings	chameleon
Fur slippers	tiger

People attempting to bring these type of products into any of the CITES member states are likely to be fined and have their purchases impounded. So, even if it looks like a harmless holiday souvenir to you, if there's any chance at all that it comes from an endangered animal (and is therefore illegal), don't buy it!

EXCESS SUNTAN

EXCESS HOLIDAY PHOTOGRAPHS

EXCESS BAGGAGE

ECO-TOURS

TESTING TIMES –
ANIMAL EXPERIMENTS

'Vivisection' originally meant cutting up live animals for scientific experiments. Today the term is used to describe experiments which cause pain, distress or harm to a living animal. Vivisection was practised by the Ancient Greeks and the Romans, but became much more widespread in Victorian times. Despite an increase in experiments (reaching an all time high in the 1970s of over 5 million experiments annually), no laws were passed on this issue until as late as 1986, with the sole exception of the 1876 Cruelty to Animals Act.

The Cruelty to Animals Act (1876) allowed licensed individuals within registered buildings to carry out animal experiments under anaesthetic, unless otherwise agreed. An 'experiment' is defined as an investigation designed to test a theory or discover something previously unknown. These experiments were to be checked by government inspectors and all animals were to be automatically killed at the end of the experiment, unless the purpose of the experiment had not been fulfilled.

The Animals (Scientific Procedures) Act was passed in 1986, allowing scientists to carry out painful procedures on animals without the risk of prosecution for cruelty. A 'procedure' is defined as an exercise to produce something (such as blood products) where the results are already known. Nothing allowed under the 1876 act was banned under the new act, despite over one hundred years having passed since its first introduction.

I PROPOSE AN EXPERIMENT TO SEE IF MONKEYS LIKE BEING EXPERIMENTED ON!

Each year, millions of live animals are used in laboratory experiments:
- to develop and test new medicines and vaccines (for both humans and animals)
- in scientific research into the workings of human and animal bodies and the diseases which affect them
- to test the safety of new cosmetics, household cleaners and industrial and agricultural chemicals (e.g. pesticides).

Much of this testing is required by law, in an effort to safeguard human health and the environment.

Animal testing is one of the most controversial of all animal rights issues with lots of conflicting views. At its centre is one key question: is it right to use animals for human benefit when the animals may suffer in the process?

Many people say that *if* animals are used:
- they should suffer as little as possible
- they should only be used if a non-animal substitute is not available
- there must be a very good reason for using them
- they should not be used to test products like cosmetics.

Animal rights activists disagree. They say that it is not possible to justify any experimentation on animals. All experiments cause pain and suffering and should be BANNED.

Animals used range from mice and rats bred specially for the laboratory, to endangered species taken from the wild, such as chimps, to pets stolen from their owners.

Mice (c. 54.5%)   Rats (c. 25%)
Rabbits and guinea pigs (10%)   Others* (10%)
Dogs and cats (0.5%)

*Others = chimps, macaque monkeys, armadillos, pigs, sheep and horses.

FACT FLASH: The first living thing in space wasn't a human being but a dog, called Laika. She was sent into orbit by the former USSR in 1957 to test the effects of space on a mammal's body. She died when her oxygen supply ran out.

Why Are Animals Used, And Not Humans?

Cancer research is one of the main areas of medical research using animals. Scientists try to recreate artificially the symptoms of the human disease in the animals by transplanting cancerous tumours into their bodies. The animals are then used to screen anti-cancer drugs or to test new types of chemotherapy.

Which sounds dreadful.

But imagine the outcry if a human being were to be used instead.

The French scientist, Claude Bernard (1813-1878), stated that *"science permits us to do to animals what morality forbids us to do to our own kind."*

Would society ever allow these sort of experiments on humans?

Who would volunteer? Would you?

Q: Which products are tested on animals?
A: Cosmetics (e.g shampoo, skin cream, make-up), house-hold products (e.g. washing-up liquid, bleach), agricultural chemicals (e.g. fertilisers, weed-killers), food additives, industrial chemicals, environmental pollutants, tobacco and alcohol.

Q: Why are they tested?
A: To see how effective they are and how safe for humans to use.

Q: Are the tests controlled by law?
A: Yes - in Britain, they're regulated by the Animals (Scientific Procedures) Act 1986. Laboratories must be licensed by the Home Office and be open to official inspection.

Q: Where do the tests take place?
A: Public health laboratories, university and hospital research laboratories, company and government laboratories.

Q: Which are the main tests involved?

A: • The Draize test - testing products on rabbits to see if they irritate the eyes or skin. The substance, e.g. shampoo, is dripped into the rabbit's eyes.

  • Skin sensitivity test - the product is applied to the shaved skin of a rabbit or guinea-pig to see if it has any side effects, such as soreness or redness.

  • Toxicity (poisoning) test - the substance is added to food or water and force-fed to mice or rats to test how poisonous it is. This is also known as the LD50 test (Lethal Dose 50%) because a product is tested to see how much of it can be taken before half of the sample of animals used dies.

Q: Do the tests cause suffering?

A: Yes, inevitably, although British labs have modified tests in recent years to reduce the suffering involved. Many tests are carried out without any anaesthetic or pain relief (though not all need them). Although anaesthetic is required by law, a special certificate can be granted if an experiment will not work with an anaesthetised animal.

Q: Don't people object to this?

A: Yes, they do. Opinion polls conducted by the RSPCA show that 95% of people are opposed to animal testing of household products and 96% to testing of cosmetics. More and more people are turning to products marked 'cruelty-free' or 'not tested on animals'. For many people, though, medical testing is a trickier matter.

Is Medical Testing Valid?

Many people agree, to an extent at least, with the use of animals in medical experiments. In their opinion, the testing of new drugs for the treatment of life-threatening diseases, such as AIDS and cancer, can be justified as essential research for the advancement of human health and science in general. Many diseases, such as polio, tuberculosis and smallpox, would still be fatal without the advances made through animal experimentation. In fact, smallpox has now been completely eradicated.

Doctors might argue that if we can prevent human suffering through scientific knowledge, we should do it. But is research always accurate - and are experiments always necessary? Many animals do not provide good models for humans and some drugs which are lethal to them, such as Aspirin and Penicillin, are vital to us, while some which cause no reaction in animals have caused side-effects in humans. And diseases like lung cancer, could, in many cases, be prevented just as well by avoiding cigarettes.

And What About Cosmetic Testing?

Should animals *ever* be used in the testing of products such as lipsticks, shampoos and soap? The majority of people say no. They argue that this is non-essential research and its use of animals is unjustifiable. Almost all cosmetic ingredients have been animal-tested at some time, and with over 8000 varieties available, there should be no need to continue testing new ingredients or products. An international campaign for a world-wide ban on animal testing in the cosmetics industry is currently underway. However, previous campaigns in 1990, 1991 and 1992 were not successful.

Psychological Testing

Some scientists believe that they can learn more about human behaviour by observing the behaviour of highly intelligent animals such as rats and monkeys.

Some animals are given electric shocks to see how stressed or aggressive they become. Others are deprived of food and water or deliberately brain damaged. Others have their babies taken from them to see how they react.

Of particular concern is the use of primates (mainly macaque monkeys and chimps). Not only does this encourage the illegal trade in wild primates (labs pay a lot of money for them), but the animals suffer terribly in their cramped laboratory cages. Chimps are used because of their genetic closeness to humans. But surely this is what makes their use so difficult to justify?

Opponents of **psychological tests** argue that they are unnecessary and cruel. Why can't scientists observe real people in real situations instead?

I'm afraid Mr. Chimp, you're finally going Bananas!

Is Animal Testing Ever Justified?

YES!

• The benefits to people outweigh any suffering to the animals.

• Without animal testing, we'll never find a cure for cancer or AIDS, two of the biggest killers of humans.

• For years, before human insulin could be produced in labs, many diabetics survived by injecting pig insulin. Otherwise they wouldn't be alive today.

• Laboratory animals are well cared for and suffering is kept to a minimum.

• There are strict laws controlling the use of animals in experiments.

• Some of the tests are useful to vets, so animals benefit from them too.

• It would be morally unacceptable to use humans instead.

Squeak
Squeak

NO!

- The pain and suffering caused to the animals cannot be justified in any circumstances.
- Tests on animals can be unreliable. Drugs suitable for animals may not be suitable for humans.
- Animal tests, especially on beauty products, are cruel and totally unnecessary.
- In laboratories, animals are kept in cramped cages and unnatural conditions.
- In many cases, the law is not enforced strictly enough to control suffering. In fact, it's the law which allows these experiments to be done in the first place!
- The illegal trade in wild-caught animals for labs is endangering the long-term survival of these species.
- In some cases, several versions of the same drug are tested unnecessarily - normally to protect companies from liability claims, *not* to protect consumers.

CLUMP
CLUMP

Alternatives To Animals

So, if animals are out, what are the alternatives?

THE 3 RS

• Reduction - reducing the number of animals used in experiments.
• Refinement - amending experiments to cause as little suffering and stress to the animals as possible.
• Replacement - finding alternative techniques for testing products' safety, rather than using animals.

Really Rotten Reptiles?

NO BOY THESE..

1. Cruelty-free products
• You can now buy many products, including cosmetics and household products, which have not been tested on animals. Find out how to be a kinder shopper on pages 112-113.

2. Computer models
• Many new drugs can now be tested using computer models, not mice. By looking at pictures of drug molecules on their computer screens, researchers can study, quickly and painlessly, how the drugs affect the body and predict any harmful side-effects.

3. Test-tube tests
• Some companies are developing new tests to replace painful animal experiments, such as the Draize test. These tests are carried out on living cells grown in test-tubes to see if products damage them. For example, a product called Eytex has been developed using a vegetable protein to mimic the human eye's reaction.

4. Database delight
• A database is being planned to allow researchers access to a central pool of experiment results, so that they will not need to perform the same experiments twice.

5. Human guinea-pigs
• People can volunteer to be human guinea-pigs for testing certain products, such as cosmetics and toiletries (finished products only). You can also donate your organs, skin and tissues to medical research so that if you die they could be used instead of laboratory animals.

6. Stay healthy!
• The fewer medicines you take, the fewer animals are used in experiments. So leading a healthy lifestyle is not only better for you but for animals too. Some people are also turning to complementary medicine, which uses natural plant products, yoga and meditation to treat illness and stress, instead of medicines tested on animals.

ENTERTAINMENT or EXPLOITATION?

Is fox-hunting fun? Are circuses degrading?
Do we need zoos? Should bullfighting be banned?

The Romans used to flock to watch gruesome wild beast shows, where animals were forced to fight each other, let loose on defenceless prisoners, or hunted by archers. In Elizabethan times, cock-fighting and bear-baiting were seen as exciting entertainment, and even today illegal dog fights and cock-fights draw large audiences. But animal rights campaigners consider the use of animals in entertainment (in its broadest sense) to be unnecessary, outdated and downright cruel. Is it really as straightforward as that? Of course not!

Take circuses for example.

Anti-circus campaigners say:
• that it is degrading to force animals to do silly tricks such as jumping through hoops.
• that the animals are punished if they don't perform.
• that circus animals spend most of their lives away from the ring, tied up, chained or in dirty, cramped cages or being transported long distances in 'beast wagons' (lorry trailers).
• that taking wild animals away from their family groups causes abnormal behaviour such as pacing up and down, head swaying and biting the bars.

Circus owners say:

• that we are transferring emotions on to animals that they wouldn't understand.

• that circuses are great entertainment, bringing pleasure to thousands of people every year.

• that they do care for their animals and look after them well.

• that most circus animals are captive-bred. They have never lived in the wild so don't miss it.

• that the animals aren't forced to do anything - they enjoy performing.

HONK HONK HONK

Zoos In The News

Many of the same arguments apply to zoos.
Here are two conflicting zoo-points.

SAVE OUR ZOOS!

• If they're well run and the animals are well
treated, zoos have a valuable role to play.
• They allow people to see animals they'd never
see otherwise. For some people living in cities,
they are their only contact with wild animals.
• They educate people about wild animals and
teach them to understand and care about them.
• They are important for conservation. Many zoos
now run **captive-breeding** programmes in which
endangered species are bred in zoos, then
reintroduced into the wild. Success stories so far
include the Arabian oryx, the Round Island boa
and the Mauritian pink pigeon. They'd all be
extinct now if zoos hadn't stepped in.
• In the best zoos, enclosures are designed to
imitate the animal's natural habitat as closely as
possible, and animals are kept in their natural
social groups wherever possible.
• A great deal of valuable research goes on
behind the scenes, where vets and
zoologists study animal behaviour,
diet and medicine.
• The keepers are devoted to the
animals and do everything they
can to make sure they're
happy and healthy.
• In some zoos, the humans
are caged, not the animals!

DOWN WITH ZOOS!

- Many pro-zoo views apply only to large, well-run, well-funded zoos. Many zoos are badly run, on a pitifully low budget.
- Wild animals belong in the wild. Keeping them in zoos is like keeping them in prison.
- However much zoos preach education and conservation, it's the entertainment factor that gets tickets sold and bills paid. So even good zoos are making money at the animals' expense.
- However 'natural' an enclosure is, it's a poor substitute for the wild. These are creatures of dense forests, open plains, vast oceans and skies.
- Not all zoos can afford or want such enclosures anyway. Some animals are kept in terrible conditions; in dark, dingy, often filthy cages - nothing like their natural homes.
- Many zoo animals show signs of **'zoochosis'**, abnormal behaviour which includes rocking or swaying from side to side, grooming themselves raw, pacing endlessly up and down, and so on. Even babies are affected. It's caused by boredom, lack of space, lack of company and an unsuitable diet.
- Reintroducing zoo-bred animals into the wild is a very risky business. They lose their instinct for survival and, unless they adapt quickly, they may die.
- Some animals, such as tigers and primates, breed well in captivity. Then there's the problem of what to do with the surplus.

Free Willy?

• The film version - the whale goes free

In the feature film, *Free Willy*, a captive orca (killer whale) is befriended and rescued from its unscrupulous owners by a young boy. And they all live happily ever after!

• The true facts - the nightmare continues

That remains to be seen. After the film, the star of the show, an Icelandic orca named Keiko, was returned to captivity - an over-small, over-warm tank in an amusement park in Mexico City. A Free Keiko campaign was quickly launched and Keiko was eventually moved to an aquarium in Oregon, USA, where he has gained weight and received medical attention. However, it is unlikely that Keiko will ever be released into the wild.

So, it's taken a film to persuade people that keeping huge, free-roaming whales in goldfish bowls is wrong! But at least it's a start. Let's hope **aquaria** – sea animal zoos – will fast be joining the ranks of endangered species.

Free Ads?

Have you seen the one where the talking chimps are advertising a well-known brand of tea?

They may be highly-trained performers but is it right to dress them up and make them act like humans? Or to laugh at them for doing so? Or is it degrading?

Animals used in adverts, films and on television are covered by strict rules and regulations. Even insects and fish. In the film, *Dances With Wolves*, fake buffalo were used in several scenes to ensure the real ones didn't get hurt. Others were trained to stampede. But it wasn't always like that. In *Apocalypse Now*, a live water buffalo was beheaded on screen.

So, is it OK to use animals on screen if they're well trained and well looked after? Or is any training too much training? Would it make a difference if these were guide dogs for the blind we were talking about, and not film extras?

FACT FLASH: In Sweden recently, a rabbit was trained to jump over hurdles. Just for a (human) laugh!

Blood Sports

Blood sports include fox-hunting, deer-hunting, shooting (e.g. game-birds and stags), angling, badger-baiting (illegal), cock-fighting (illegal) and dog-fighting (illegal). Hunting, shooting and fishing are left-overs from the days when people had to hunt to eat. This is no longer necessary now that farms produce most of our food, so these sports are now pursued for pleasure instead. Millions of mammals and birds are killed for sport each year.

Many people find the very idea of killing animals for sport disgusting and want **blood sports** banned. The hunters disagree.

In the fox-hunting debate, there are three sides (at least) to the story. Each year about 18,000 foxes are killed by packs of dogs, with riders in hot pursuit. A typical hunt consists of as many as sixty horses and hounds...
versus one fox!

THE FARMER speaks:
- Foxes are pests which prey on farmers' stock. They must be controlled.
- They're vicious killers, attacking lambs and chickens.
- They can cost struggling farmers hundreds of pounds a year.
- The people who object to fox-hunting are usually townies who don't understand the ways of the countryside.

THE HUNTER speaks:
- Fox-hunting is a traditional country sport hundreds of years old.
- The farmers would shoot the foxes anyway.
- The hounds are trained to go straight for the throat, so death is almost instantaneous.
- Hunting is great exercise and we enjoy it!

THE FOX speaks:

• Foxes actually kill very few lambs or chickens.

• Hunting is extremely cruel. The night before the hunt, foxes' earths (burrows) are often blocked up to keep the foxes above ground.

• Once the hounds smell a fox, they chase it to the point of exhaustion, then kill it. The hunt can last for several hours before the fox is killed.

• If the fox goes to ground, terriers are sent in to drag it out.

• Pregnant and nursing vixen (females) are often the victims.

• Public opinion seems to support a ban on fox-hunting.

FACT FLASH: Did you know that every time someone goes to a local horse race or point-to-point, they are contributing towards fox-hunting through their entrance fee, as these events are organised by local hunts?

Like A Red Rag...

Which 'sport' involves the following:

• Spears stabbed into the animal's neck?
• Vaseline smeared in the animal's eyes to blur its vision?
• Animals taunted with capes and lances?

You've guessed it - it's BULLFIGHTING.

In Spain, bullfights are big business, with ticket sales worth millions of pounds a year. Many of the spectators are tourists. And this is what they pay to see...

The bull is released into the ring. It's been kept in darkness and is dazzled and confused by the light. It's goaded with red capes and speared in the neck with lances until it cannot lift its head. Only then does the matador (bullfighter) enter the ring for the kill. He aims his sword between the bull's shoulder blades and into its heart. This first blow rarely kills the bull - another five or six attempts may be needed. It's a slow and painful death.

Despite a growing movement to ban bullfights, they seem to be getting more popular. For supporters of bullfights, they are part of Spain's tradition and culture, and are a display of human courage and skill. For opponents, they're blood-thirsty, barbaric and totally unnecessary.

So what do you think? Is it cruelty or culture?

FACT FLASH: At some fun fairs in Spain, real ponies are used as roundabout rides, attached to automated machines with blaring music and flashing lights, and sent round and round in continuous circles.

JUST WHY ARE PETS SO POPULAR?

Have you got a pet? Has it got a name? Do you talk to it as if it were human? Would you be very upset if it died?

Millions of people have pets. But why? Is it because they don't answer back? Or because they're good company? Or because they make us feel wanted and needed? Do we, in fact, treat them more like people-substitutes than animals?

Some animal rights campaigners argue that keeping animals as pets is wrong - another form of exploitation. It's also cruel. Budgerigars, for example, should be flying free in the forests of Australia, not being cooped up in tiny cages in people's living rooms. And hamsters travel up to 8 km a night in their natural desert habitat, while we keep them in tiny cages with only a wheel to exercise on.

AAH SQUIDY... I LOVE you!

Then there's our attitude to animals in general. Not all animals arouse the same feelings in people. Some seem easier to like than others. The sight of a puppy, kitten or furry seal cub, for example, makes us 'ooh' and 'aah' and feel instantly protective. This irresistible appeal is called the 'cuddle factor'. For example, you might eat chicken. But you'd never eat your cuddly pet cat, would you?

So, are we a nation of animal-lovers or a bunch of hypocrites?

It's Official - Cats Are Top...Cats!

Until very recently, dogs were our most popular pets, with twelve dogs to every 100 people in Britain (in Germany it's four per 100 and in the USA it's twenty five!) Cats used to come a close second, but, according to the latest Social Trends survey, they have now overtaken dogs to take first place, with 7 million cats living in Britain, compared to 6.5 million dogs.

There are also millions of pet birds, fish, hamsters, gerbils, rabbits, mice and guinea pigs. Not to mention horses, ponies and tortoises...

At its best, our relationship with pets benefits both sides. Pets get food, shelter and attention. Owners get companionship, hours of fun, protection (sometimes) and something to stroke (said to reduce stress).

N° 2?   N° 1?   N° 3?

But if we're really such doting pet-owners, how come we've got such a bad record of cruelty to the animals we keep?

• About a thousand dogs are put down every week. Many are either unwanted presents, abandoned when they get too big or too costly to feed; or unwanted puppies, born as a result of owners not bothering to get their animals spayed. Cats suffer in the same way.
• Since 1989, convictions for cruelty to dogs have risen by 60%.
• Acts of cruelty include skinning cats alive, drowning puppies, flushing kittens down toilets, dumping unwanted animals along motorways and even microwaving kittens.
• Pets are also stolen for sale to research laboratories, to the fur trade (e.g. tabby cats) and to the meat trade (e.g. horses and ponies).
• Feeding pets on unsuitable food (e.g. ponies being fed on cornflakes and rice pudding; hamsters being fed pork sausages) leads to infection, lameness and bone deformities. Some pets are even deliberately starved by their owners.

I ain't no Santa claus...

KITTENS and PUPPIES

Horrible, isn't it? But it's not just cruelty that kills. It's just as bad to give pets *too* much food and pampering. In fact, in 1996, the UK had the fattest pets in Europe! Which means we also had... Pet Slimmer of the Year! That year's winner won his owner a foreign holiday, while all he got was a lousy dog bowl! It's a dog's life...

DO YOUR FRIENDS LAUGH AT YOUR LITTLE FAT DOG? DO THEY GIGGLE AT YOUR GLUTTONOUS KITTY?
Then Try

PET-SLIM-PLUS

Man's best friend also seems to get the worst of it from another point of view. Dogs are often subjected to operations by their owners which seem cruel and unnecessary, like tail-docking (where a young dog's tail is cut off), ear-cropping (when a dog's ears are trimmed for fashion) and de-barking (where a dog's vocal cords are cut to prevent it causing a disturbance). And it's not only dogs - cats are often de-clawed (to prevent damage to furniture!).

Tail-docking is an area which has aroused lots of strong feelings, both from its opponents and its promoters.

• **Advantages** - Owners and vets who support tail-docking argue that it prevents injuries, such as broken tails, later on in life, particularly in dogs used for field-sports (like gun-dogs). It also prevents shaggier breeds (like Old English sheepdogs) from becoming soiled around the rear, which in turn prevents problems of hygiene.

• **Disadvantages** - The operation is carried out without an anaesthetic, even though it involves cutting through bone and arteries. Puppies may have the operation when they are newborn, but this doesn't stop them feeling pain.

In 1992, The Royal College of Veterinary Surgeons banned all vets from carrying out docking operations unless there was a proper medical reason for it. But some vets still continue this practice, while some owners carry the procedure out themselves (illegally) or even send their dogs abroad for docking.

Opponents of tail-docking argue that it is most often carried out for purely cosmetic reasons, by owners who show their dogs, and is of no real benefit to the dog.

Owners who show their animals or breed them, sometimes do more harm than good, when their animal's appearance becomes more important than its health. In some cases this means breeding animals especially to match the judges' exacting requirements.

But 'designer' cats have health problems that your normal moggy would never experience - like cats whose noses are set so far back in their heads that they can't breathe properly, or the poor hairless Sphynx cat, which, without a protective layer of fur, is easily injured by scratches, the cold or strong sunlight.

They say that cats have nine lives - if we're not careful they might end up with nine heads!

The Exotic Pet Trade

For some people, cats and dogs aren't enough. They want more exotic pets like snakes, macaws, even big cats. It's a growing craze. And its effect on wild populations of often endangered species is devastating.

For example:

Born to be wild - parrots and macaws

• Every year, more than 5 million wild birds are traded as pets. And for every bird that makes it, three die in transit. And this is before you count the illegal trade in endangered species. Parrots and macaws have been worst hit. The trade in African grey parrots has decimated wild populations. In Mexico, illegal trafficking has reduced the number of yellow naped parrots by 90% in the last twenty years. The number of Spix macaws in the wild now stands at a grand total of...ONE! The list goes on and on.

• Most of the parrots you see in pet shops have been captured from the wild. NEVER even *think* about buying one. If you *must* have a parrot, make sure it's been captive-bred.

• Many major airlines now refuse to transport wild-caught birds. The call for a worldwide ban of this trade continues.

The Great Ninja Turtle Disaster

• Animals go in and out of fashion just like clothes - but just because an animal is 'in' doesn't mean it will make a good pet. A case in point is the Ninja Turtle craze of the early nineties which was bad news for red-eared terrapins. The most widely traded pet reptile, about 200,000 are imported into Britain each year, from special terrapin breeding ranches in the USA. The trouble is that breeding stocks are kept up by taking animals from the wild. The greater the demand, the more wild animals are caught. (Before each Christmas, demand for live 'Ninja' turtles grew by 400%!) To make matters worse, up to 99% of terrapins die in their first year of captivity, mainly from unnatural causes. In the wild, they usually live about 30 years.

• A total of 4-7 million red-eared terrapins are exported from the USA each year.

• In the USA itself, you can't keep terrapins as pets because they often carry the salmonella bacteria which can make you ill!

•If in doubt, stick to cats and dogs. Exotic pets need exotic food and care - things most owners can't provide.

ONE OF THEM IS BOUND TO LAST UNTIL TOMORROW!

SHAKE

1000's TURTLES

How Much Is That Doggy In The Window?

If you're thinking of getting a pet, beware!
Ask yourself a few searching questions first:

1. Can you give it a good home?
(A 10th floor flat is not suitable for a cat.)
2. Can you afford it?
(Pet food can be expensive if you're on a
tight budget, and vets' bills are a big cost too.)
3. Can you spend time with it?
(It's not fair if you're out all day.)
4. Can you give it enough exercise?
(Dogs need walking regularly.)
5. Can you have it looked after if you're away?
(A kind friend or neighbour may
not always be available, and kennels
and catteries cost money.)
6. Are you ready to look after it for the rest of
its life?
(Dogs can live for 15 years; cats for up to 20.)

If the answer to any of these is NO, think again.

If the answer is YES,
• try your local animal rescue or the RSPCA for a
pet in need of a good home - you'll have a friend
for life!
• steer clear of pet shops. Any puppies you see
may come from puppy farms, where they're often
bred in terrible conditions. In addition, they may
not have had vital vaccinations, despite the
shop-owner's claims, and may die from potentially
fatal diseases such as parvo-virus.

And, Finally...

Scientists in the USA are designing a personality test for kittens which predicts how they'll turn out as adults. The aim is to help people choose a pet to suit them. There are three categories - lap cat (friends with everyone), wild cat (watch out, mice!) and timid cat (the wouldn't-say-'Boo'-to-a-goose type). So far, however, there are no plans for a similar test for potential cat owners!

DILINI WANTS A CAT TO CUDDLE.

CARL WANTS A CAT THAT WILL PLAY WITH HIS SHOELACES.

JANICE WANTS A CAT TO HELP HER WITH HER HOMEWORK.

PAUL WANTS A CAT TO BE HIS BEST FRIEND.

ROSHAN WANTS A CAT THAT NEVER STOPS PURRING.

BILLY WANTS A CAT BECAUSE HIS SISTER IS ALLERGIC TO THEM.

LIFE-SAVER OR LUXURY?

You've read about the issues and debated the problems, but where does all this leave us? Much as we'd like to, can we afford to acknowledge that animals have rights?

Even if we can, can we really expect people in Third World countries, often living in abject poverty, to share our concern for animal welfare when they themselves don't get enough to eat?

Can we expect people to care about animals in countries where their own human rights are denied?

Or is the whole issue of animal rights a luxury, only possible in the wealthy West where people can afford to care?

And are we right to try to impose our views on different countries and different cultures? Shouldn't we sort out our own attitude towards animals first?

What do YOU think?

THE FUTURE

MOVEMENTS FOR ANIMAL RIGHTS

More than 170 years since its foundation, the RSPCA is still going strong, with its efforts concentrated on four main areas of concern - farming, wildlife, animal experimentation and companion animals (pets). Originally based on Christian principles, the RSPCA is highly respected and very popular. Animal welfare is now centre stage, and a variety of other groups have sprung up to champion the cause. Among them are campaigners with an altogether more radical agenda.

Direct Action

The Animal Liberation Front (ALF) started life as a group called the Band of Mercy. In the 1970s, it began a campaign of direct action on behalf of animals: freeing animals from laboratories and factory farms; sabotaging research work; stealing documents and generally exposing the conditions animals were kept in.

Today their aims remain the same. The Animal Liberation Front carries out raids itself or through a number of well-organised, undercover splinter groups, such as the aggressively named Animal Rights Militia.

The reason these groups are undercover is because what they're doing is illegal. An animal rights **activist** was recently jailed for 10 years for organising a nationwide bombing campaign. Targets included labs, cars owned by research scientists and department stores selling fur.

But does this extremist attitude actually help the cause of animal rights? Or does it do more harm than good?

Most animal welfare groups condemn the violence and distance themselves from this 'warrior' attitude, branded as terrorism by many. There are, they argue, many equally effective, non-violent ways of protesting against cruelty to animals. Violence has no future.

Greenpeace is an environmental group which believes in non-violent protests on a variety of issues. One of their most prominent concerns is whaling. The International Whaling Commission (IWC) is currently overseeing a ban on commercial whaling. But Norway continues whaling, and has, in fact, doubled its whaling quota in 1996, a quota that now stands at 425 minke whales annually. There is currently a ban on Norway exporting the resulting whalemeat, but there is a fear that the whalers will manage to overturn this ruling. If so, Greenpeace and other environmental groups are going to have their work cut out for them. And whales will be even more under threat.

What does the future hold for *these* species of animals? Will *they* live to see the future? It seems highly unlikely. By the year 2000, they could all be extinct...

1. **Golden bamboo lemur** (Madagascar)
Threat: burning of forest habitat
* Only discovered in 1987.

2. **Mediterranean Monk seal**
Threat: human disturbance (including tourism)
* Also persecuted by fishermen.

3. **Yangtze River Dolphin** (China)
Threat: damming of river, collision with boats
* Fewer than 100 left.

4. **Californian condor** (USA)
Threat: shooting, lead poisoning
* Extinct in the wild since 1987; now only bred in captivity.

5. **Chinese alligator**
Threat: habitat loss, hunting, capture for zoos and farms
* Main hope of survival is the development of breeding farms.

6. **Saint Helena giant earwig** (South Atlantic)
Threat: habitat disruption
* The world's largest earwig. Last seen in 1967.

It is estimated that between 1975 and 2000, one million species will have died out for ever.

ANIMAL
COFFINS
MADE TO
ORDER

GENE JUGGLING

When is a sheep not a sheep?
When it's a geep, of course!

While some species are dying out, new species are being created. A geep is a cross between a goat and a sheep, produced by **genetic engineering**, one of the latest and most controversial technological breakthroughs. Genes are responsible for an animal's characteristics. By altering them, scientists can alter an animal's size, shape and appearance.

It's amazing what genetics can do!

The 'Crabbit'
½ Cow ½ Rabbit

ACTUAL SIZE!

mini Bite-Sized Chicken

NOT ACTUAL SIZE!

Giant Milk Cows

The 'Peep'
½ Sheep ½ Pig

Q: So, how can genetic engineering be used?

A: • to produce new medicines for humans and an

   • to produce bigger animals for increased production.

   • to produce pigs whose hearts are suitable for transplanting into humans (see page 108).

   • to produce the growth hormone BST which increases the amount of milk cows produce.

   • to reduce the number of animals used, e.g. the same amount of rennet can now be genetically engineered from one calf, as was originally taken from many.

Q: What are the concerns?

A: • in the wrong hands, it could get out of control with extremely sinister consequences.

   • it has already had freak results e.g. giant lambs and calves.

   • introducing 'foreign' genes into animals can have unpredictable side effects e.g. arthritis in pigs - and cows treated with BST suffer painful udder infections.

   • animals should not be tampered with for human benefit (exploitation again).

   • animals shouldn't be turned into chemical factories.

   • genetically engineered meat may not be safe to eat.

   • in the USA new genetic mixes are licensed or patented as inventions. This degrades animals and reduces them to machines.

   • what right have scientists to play God?

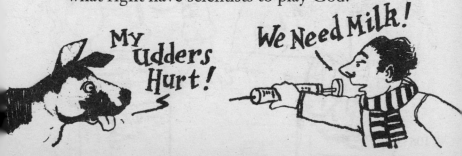

Animal Transplants

Try to imagine the situation. You desperately need a kidney transplant but there are no human donors available. An animal kidney is offered instead. But you feel strongly about animals rights. Do you take the kidney or refuse it?

The use of animals organs for human transplants, called **xenotransplants**, is still in its very early stages. The very first experiments in the 1960s with sheep hearts proved unsuccessful. Today, pigs are being genetically engineered to reduce the risk of their organs (kidneys and hearts) being rejected if transplanted into humans. And, although the transplant of animal organs into humans is currently banned in the UK because of the fear of animal viruses passing to humans, surgeons hope the procedure will be routine by 2001.

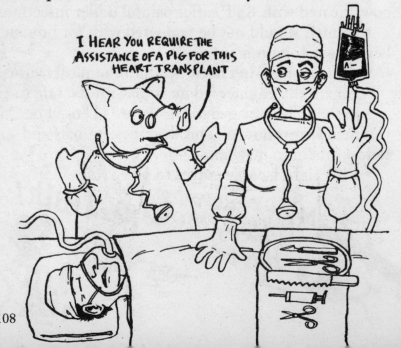

Why are xenotransplants necessary? The answer is simple - there just aren't enough human organs to go round. Over 6000 people are on the waiting list for transplant operations in the UK, more than can be operated on annually - in fact, only 50 heart and lung transplants are carried out each year in the UK.

The main scientific worries about xenotransplants is the risk of animal organs carrying new infectious diseases into humans. Before human trials can begin, a rigorous screening programme must be put into place. And the whole process must be tightly controlled and monitored.

And while pigs might be acceptable, what about primates? Where should we draw the line? In the USA, baboon organs, including bone marrow, have already been transplanted into humans (with little success). Because of their genetic closeness to humans, the risk of disease is greater. Because of their genetic closeness to humans, should they be used at all? Animal rights activists object to the use of animal organs as 'spare parts' for humans - particularly as the animals used are bred especially for this purpose.

So, what would you do? Is this another form of animal exploitation, to be placed alongside testing, the fur trade, circuses and fox-hunting? Or do things change when it's a matter of life and death - particularly your own?

THE RISE OF THE VEGETARIAN

Self-interest also seems to have played a part in the astounding conversion of over one million people to vegetarianism between spring 1995 and spring 1996. This was due to the disclosures about BSE and fear about the connection between its human equivalent, CJD, and eating beef.

However, the more people become vegetarian, for whatever reason, the more influence the vegetarian lobby will have. Supermarkets such as Sainsbury and Tesco already produce a wide range of vegetarian foods in consultation with the Vegetarian Society - and now the Vegetarian Society is campaigning against supermarkets stocking 'exotic' meats such as kangaroo, crocodile or ostrich, or encouraging the 'exotic' meat trade, because of the cruelties involved.

WATCH THEY DON'T 'JUMP' OUT THE PAN, huh huh huh

PLAIN PORK

PRIME GIRAFFE

ORGANIC CAMEL

OSTRICH STEAK

KANGAROO SAUSAGE

Shopping Without Shocking

One of the ways in which you *can* show your (peaceful) concern for animal rights is by becoming a cruelty-free shopper. This means choosing from the wide (and growing) range of food, cosmetics and other products which haven't been tested on animals, don't contain animal ingredients or haven't been factory farmed.

First, you need to know what you're looking for:

Freedom Food - meat or dairy products which carry this label are endorsed by the RSPCA. 'Freedom food' means the producers of the food have agreed to make a commitment to animal welfare at all stages of the animal's life, from birth to slaughter.

Free-range - eggs labelled 'free-range' or 'barn (perchery) eggs' are those laid by hens which are allowed to wander freely outside or live in flocks inside large buildings, with nest boxes and perches for roosting on.

Dolphin-friendly - if you eat tuna, check for this label. It means that the fish were caught using poles and lines, rather than drift nets which can trap and kill dolphins and other sea-creatures.

Vegetarian - look for the Vegetarian Society's green 'V' on food products. This means that it is suitable for vegetarians to eat and doesn't contain meat or fish.

Cruelty-free – means that a product contains no animal ingredients, and neither the product nor the ingredients have been tested on animals.

Not tested on animals – means this particular version of the product has not been tested on animals. The original, prototype version may well have been, however.

But BEWARE! Look at the labels carefully. Some can be misleading, e.g. Not tested on animals does not *necessarily* mean cruelty-free and Farm Fresh, Country Fresh and Traditional eggs may actually be produced by battery hens. Other products may claim to be cruelty-free when they're not. At present there is no legal definition of terms, and different companies are free to base their claims on different criteria. If in doubt, there are various books to help you (see page 126). The RSPCA also produces an approved products guide.

CAN YOU MATCH THE PRODUCT TO THE BASKET?

115

BEAT THOSE HOLIDAY BLUES - GO GREEN!

What do you look for in a holiday? Sun? Sea? Sand? Unique wildlife? Unspoilt wilderness? Unbelievable views?

If it's the last three you're after, you might count yourself as an 'eco-tourist' - the latest buzz word to describe people who want to see the world but also want the world to survive being seen. Tourism is a growing industry, bringing much needed income to many of the world's poorer countries. But so many people now want to visit, they're harming the environment, the local people and the wildlife. Many travel companies now run eco-friendly holidays which aim to reduce the impact of tourists on wild places. The question is - can these places survive our interest in the future, however well-intentioned it is?

Turtle Beach hotel

So Where Is This Rare Turtle Breedi Ground Exactly?

The Hotel Is Built On It Sir!

WILD LIFE GUIDE

ECO VALET

YES!

• Local people can benefit from tourism if it is well managed and if their needs and feelings are taken into account.

• If local people, skills and resources are involved, the chances of any conservation efforts succeeding are much greater.

• Eco-tourism has huge educational potential.

• The demand for green holidays shows people's growing concern for the environment.

NO!

• In Bali, raw sewage from tourist hotels is dumped into the sea, destroying coral reefs and beaches.

• To construct an airport on the idyllic island of Cebu in the Philippines, five coral islands were destroyed.

• Nepal's mountain streams are being polluted by trekkers' rubbish (including large amounts of toilet paper).

• No one knows for sure what long-term effect the disruption caused by tourists (however minimal) will have on local wildlife. Already koalas in Australia have shown signs of stress after being cuddled by tourists (this is now banned).

HOME, SWEET HOME?

When pets are brought back into Britain after living abroad, they are subject to **quarantine** laws which see them locked up in kennels for six months before they are returned to their owners.

These laws were introduced in Britain in 1901 and were used to prevent the spread of rabies in the UK. They are currently the strictest laws in the world. Approximately 1 in every 60 animals dies during this period in kennels, more often from stress or neglect than from rabies. In fact, there has not been a single reported case of a rabid animal in quarantine since 1969.

Because of the high incidence of deaths while in isolation, and the high costs involved in kennelling pets (£2000 for each animal in quarantine) the number of animals being smuggled back into the UK has increased.

HOW LONG ARE YOU IN FOR YOUNG PUP?

SIX MONTHS

People are now protesting that the quarantine laws are out of date and unnecessary. A group called Passports for Pets  suggests that a passport system for animals would be equally successful in preventing the spread of rabies. Pets would carry a microchip implant to prove their identity and their 'passports' would prove that they have had their rabies vaccination. A similar system has been running successfully in Sweden since 1994 and has resulted in a drop in animal smuggling.

Campaigners are pushing for Britain to switch from quarantine to pet passports and more and more people are beginning to agree. It is likely that the RSPCA will endorse this decision and help lobby the government for change. The government has already begun looking at alternatives, such as cutting the quarantine period to one month only. So watch this space!!

AND SO...

For animals everywhere, the future is uncertain. Unless we change our attitudes towards them, and our treatment of them, many will have no future.

But it's not all gloom and doom. Animal rights is one of the hottest topics of the moment, firmly in the forefront of people's minds. And it's destined to stay there for a long time to come.

YOU CAN HELP

If you are concerned about animal rights and want to help, here are 10 top tips for things to do.

1. DO buy free-range and organic eggs and meat, instead of factory-farmed products. They're a bit more expensive but they're much better for you - and for the animals.

2. DO try eating vegetarian food for a couple of days each week, even if you can't give up meat altogether. There are masses of simple and delicious recipes to tantalise your taste-buds.

3. DO choose alternatives to leather and fur when you're buying shoes and clothes. There are lots of trendy, synthetic alternatives.

4. DON'T buy any holiday souvenirs which might come from endangered species. That way you won't encourage illegal trade.

5. DON'T buy cosmetics or toiletries which have been tested on animals. Choose cruelty-free products instead.

6. DO think again if you're going to a circus or marine park. And if you *are* going to the zoo, make sure it's a good zoo, committed to education and conservation and with a good track record of animal care.

7. **DON'T** take part in any blood sports. And discourage anyone you know from hunting and shooting. If you're in Spain, boycott the bullfights.

8. **DO** look after your pets and keep them properly fed, watered and exercised. Don't buy puppies or kittens from pet shops - they may have been churned out of a puppy farm and are more likely to have physical or psychological problems because of the poor conditions they're kept in.

9. **DO** tell someone if you witness an act of cruelty. Jot down as many details as you can remember, then phone your local branch of the RSPCA. Don't interfere yourself - you might get hurt.

10. **DO** make your views known. Write to your MP, your local newspaper, council or even your local supermarket manager if there's something you feel strongly about. Keep the letter short, polite and clear. Or join an animal welfare organisation - many have special groups for young people (see the list on page 127).

Now try the quiz on pages 22-23 again! You might have changed your mind...

Animal Rights And The Law - Some Key Dates

1876 The Cruelty to Animals Act
• Aim: the licensing and regulation of animal experiments; not replaced until 1986 by which time it was hopelessly out of date.
1911 The Protection of Animals Act
• Aim: the prohibition of cruelty and unnecessary suffering to animals.
1925 The Performing Animals (Regulation) Act
• Aim: the licensing and regulation of all animal trainers.
1934 The Protection of Animals Act
• Aim: to forbid rodeos in Britain because of the cruelty to the horses and bulls involved.
1937 The Cinematograph Films (Animals) Act
• Aim: to prevent the suffering of animals in films; wild animals are excluded, except those in captivity.
1949 The Docking and Nicking of Horses Act (1949)
• Aim: to stop the practice of cutting off horses' tails; this was originally to prevent the tails getting caught in the harness or carriage but is no longer necessary.
1951/1983 The Pet Animals Act
• Aim: the licensing of all pet shops; it also bans the sale of pets in streets or any public place.
1954 The Protection of Animals (Anaesthetics) Act
• Aim: all animals must be anaesthetised before operations to stop them feeling any pain.
1954 The Pests Act
• Aim: to ban the sale, possession or use of most spring-traps to kill or catch animals, such as rabbits.
1960 The Abandonment of Animals Act
• Aim: to prevent the abandonment of animals for any length of time, in circumstances likely to cause them suffering, unless there is a reasonable excuse.
1962 The Animals (Cruel Poisons) Act
• Aim: to stop people laying poisons to kill domestic animals; once again, wild animals are excluded.
1968 The Agriculture (Miscellaneous Provisions) Act
• Aim: to prevent unnecessary suffering to animals used in farming and for food.
1976 The Dangerous Wild Animals Act
• Aim: to ban the keeping of dangerous animals (as pets, for example) without a licence.

1981 The Wildlife and Countryside Act
• Aim: to protect wild animals in their wild habitats.
1981 The Zoo Licensing Act
• Aim: to make sure that zoo animals are properly cared for and do not present a danger to the public; zoos have to be inspected before a licence to operate may be granted.
1986 The Animals (Scientific Procedures) Act
• Aim: to update the 1876 Act and seek to ensure the welfare of animals used in medical and scientific experiments.
1987 The Protection of Animals (Penalties) Act
• Aim: to increase the penalties imposed by the 1911 Act.
1988 The Protection of Animals (Amendment) Act
• Act: to strengthen the 1911 Act further but allowing a court to disqualify a person from keeping animals on a first conviction cruelty.
1988 The Protection Against Cruel Tethering Act
• Aim: to ban the tying up of horses and donkeys without adequate shelter, food and water.
1991 The Dangerous Dogs Act
• Aim: to protect people from dangerous dogs; the court can order dangerous dogs to be muzzled, or even put down.
1991 The Badgers Act
• Aim: to protect badgers, especially from dogs used in the illegal 'sport' of badger-baiting.
1991 The Breeding of Dogs Act
• Aim: to stop unlicensed dog breeding on so-called 'puppy farms'.
1991 The Deer Act
• Aim: to prevent the unlicensed hunting and poaching of deer and sale of venison.
1996 The Wild Mammals (Protection Bill)
• Aim: to prevent cruelty to wild creatures unless it is for a legitimate sport. People now risk a maximum fine of £5000 or six months imprisonment if they "mutilate, kick, beat, nail or otherwise impale, stab, burn, stone, crush, drown, drag or asphyxiate any wild mammal".
STOP PRESS: In 1997 bills are being proposed to amend the Dangerous Dogs' Act, to prevent many innocent dogs being put down unnecessarily - and to add to the Breeding and Sale of Dogs Bill, so that RSPCA and local authority powers are increased, allowing them to clamp down on the black market and improve conditions on legal puppy farms.

Glossary

abattoir - a slaughterhouse, where animals are killed for their meat.

activists - people who take action on behalf of animals, either in the form of protests or, in more extreme cases, deliberate sabotage of laboratories and so on.

animal rights - the belief that all animals have the moral right to be treated with respect and without exploitation.

animal welfare - animal welfare campaigners seek the best possible conditions for, and treatment of, animals.

aquaria - sea animal zoos containing whales, sharks, sea-lions and dolphins, amongst others.

battery hens - egg-laying hens kept in tiny wire cages stacked many rows high inside a large shed.

blood sports - sports which involve the killing of animals.

captive-bolt method - a means of stunning animals before slaughter, by a bullet to the brain.

captive-breeding - the breeding of endangered species in captivity, with a view to reintroducing them into the wild.

cosmetics - products such as shampoos, hairsprays, soaps, face creams, deodorants and make-up.

culled - killing weaker or older animals off to keep numbers down.

endangered - animals faced with becoming extinct unless action is taken to save them.

extinction - when a species of animal dies out for ever.

factory farming - an intensive farming method used to mass-produce food from animals. Animals are kept indoors in cramped pens or cages while they are fattened up for slaughter.

fur farms - 'farms' which raise animals, such as mink and fox, in small, cramped cages, specifically for their fur.

genetic engineering - a biological technique in which genes are moved from one species to another to speed up growth, alter shape and size and even create brand new species.

organic - food (animal or vegetable) which is produced without the use of chemical pesticides or fertilisers.

psychological tests - experiments to test an animal's behaviour, such as how they cope with stress, isolation, starvation and so on.

quarantine - keeping animals, such as dogs, locked up in isolation when they come into the country from abroad, in order to prevent the spread of contagious diseases, such as rabies.

speciesism - discriminating against animals and treating them as inferior to humans.

sticking - a method of slaughtering cattle by hoisting them up by their hind legs and cutting their throats.

vegan - someone who avoids all animal produce or products tested on animals, including eggs, honey, milk and leather.

vegetarian - someone who does not eat meat, fish or poultry or any foods that involve killing animals.

vivisection - the use of live animals in experiments.

xenotransplants - the transplanting of animal organs, such as sheep hearts and pigs' kidneys, into humans.

zoochosis - abnormal behaviour, such as rocking or swaying, seen in some zoo animals, particularly those kept in cramped, unnatural conditions.

Further Reading
If you would like to find out more about some of the issues raised in this book, these books will provide additional information.

General:
The Young Person's Action Guide to Animal Rights
by Barbara James (Virago)
The Animal Welfare Handbook
by Caroline Clough and Barry Kew (Fourth Estate)
The Pocketbook of Animal Facts and Figures
by Barry Kew (Green Print)
Survival: Animal Rights by Miles Barton (Watts)
The Animal Contract by Desmond Morris (Virgin)
Save the Animals! 101 easy things you can do by Ingrid Newkirk (Angus & Robertson)
In Defence of Animals edited by Peter Singer (Blackwell)
Animal Liberation by Peter Singer (Thorsons)
Why Animal Rights? (Animal Aid)
Animal Rights and Human Wrongs by Sid Jenkins (Lennard Publishing)

Cruelty-free living:
The Cruelty-Free Shopper by Lis Howlett (Bloomsbury)
The Kind Food Guide by Audrey Eyton (Penguin)
The Green Consumer Guide by John Elkington and
Julia Hailes (Gollancz)
First Steps in Vegetarian Cooking by Kathy Silk (The Vegetarian Society)
The Young Vegetarian's A-Z by Debra Shipley
The Teenage Vegetarian Survival Guide by Anouchka Grose
Living Without Cruelty by Mark Gold (Green Print)

Sport, Entertainment and Pets:
Zoo 2000: A look behind the bars by Jeremy Cherfas (BBC)
Beyond the Bars edited by Virginia McKenna, William Travers and Jonathan Wray (Thorsons)
The Rose-tinted Menagerie by William Johnson (Heretic Books)
Finding out about Country Sports by Robin Page (Hobsons)
In the Company of Animals by James Serpell (Blackwell)

Wildlife and Environment:
Ecology by Richard Spurgeon (Usborne)
The Young Person's Guide to Saving the Planet
by Debbie Silver and Bernadette Vallely (Virago)
Close to Extinction by John Burton (Watts)
The Atlas of Endangered Species by John Burton (David & Charles)

Animal Experiments:
Why Animal Experiments Must Stop by Vernon Coleman (Green Print)
The Ethical Scientist (Animal Aid)
What is Vivisection? (British Union for the Abolition of Vivisection)
The Cruel Deception: The Use of Animals in Medical Research
by Robert Sharpe (Thorsons)

Useful addresses

Animal Aid (incorporating **Chicken's Lib**)
7 Castle Street, Tonbridge
Kent TN9 1BH
Tel: 01732 364546
Campaigns against all forms of animal abuse, especially vivisection and factory farming, through its Living Without Cruelty message.

Animal Liberation Front (ALF)
BM Box 4400, London WC1N 3XX
Tel: 01954 30542
Campaigns through direct action against animal abuse.

Beauty Without Cruelty
57 King Henry's Walk,
London N1 4NH
Tel: 0171 254 2929
Aims to make people aware of cruelty inflicted on animals for the sake of fashion.

British Union for the Abolition of Vivisection
16a Crane Grove, Islington,
London N7 8LB
Tel: 0171 700 4888
Aims to end experiments on living animals.

Compassion in World Farming
Charles House, 5a Charles Street
Petersfield, Hants GU32 3EH
Tel: 01730 260791
Campaigns to end factory farming and protect animals on farms.

Environmental Investigation Agency (EIA)
2 Pear Tree Court
London EC1R 0DS
Tel: 0171 490 7040
Works to conserve and protect wildlife and the environment.

The Farm and Food Society
4 Willifield Way, London NW11 7XT
Tel: 0181 455 0634
Aims to promote humane farming techniques, in harmony with the environment.

Fund for the Replacement of Animals in Medical Experiments (FRAME)
Eastgate House, 34 Stoney Street
Nottingham NG1 1NB
Tel: 0115 9584740
Aims to reduce live animal experiments and develop alternative methods.

Greenpeace
Canonbury Villas, London N1 2PN
Tel: 0171 865 8100

International Fund for Animal Welfare (IFAW)
Tubwell House, New Road
Crowborough, East Sussex TN6 2QH
Tel: 01892 601900

International Primate Protection League
116 Judd Street, London WC1H 9NS
Tel: 0171 837 7227

League Against Cruel Sports
83-87 Union Street, London SE1 1SG
Tel: 0171 403 6155
Campaigns to abolish blood sports.

National Petwatch
PO Box 16, Brighouse
West Yorkshire HD6 1DS
Tel: 01484 722411
Aims to protect pets from cruelty and suffering.

People for the Ethical Treatment of Animals (PETA)
PO Box 3169, London NW1 2JF
Tel: 0181 785 3113

Royal Society for the Prevention of Cruelty to Animals (RSPCA)
Causeway, Horsham
West Sussex RH12 1HG
Tel: 01403 64181

Royal Society for the Protection of Birds (RSPB)
The Lodge, Sandy
Bedfordshire SG19 2DL
Tel: 01767 680551

The Vegetarian Society
Parkdale, Dunham Road, Altrincham
Cheshire WA14 4QG
Tel: 0161 928 0793

World Society for the Protection of Animals
1A Park Place, Lawn Lane
London SW8 1UA
Tel: 0171 793 0540

Worldwide Fund for Nature (WWF)
Panda House, Weyside Park
Godalming, Surrey GU7 7RX
Tel: 01483 426444

Zoo Check (incorporating **Born Free** and **Elefriends**)
Cherry Tree Cottage, Coldharbour
Dorking, Surrey RH5 6HA
Tel: 01306 712091
Aims to check and prevent abuse to captive animals.

INDEX